Deborah Miller is 49 years old and lives just outside Glasgow in a place called Cumbernauld. She is married and the mother of two adult children, a boy and a girl. She has studied social sciences and human biology and now devotes her time to writing children's stories. She has always enjoyed writing as a hobby for her kids and now wants to share her stories with others.

I Need Re-Wired

Deborah Miller

Austin Macauley Publishers™
LONDON • CAMBRIDGE • NEW YORK • SHARJAH

Copyright © Deborah Miller 2023

The right of **Deborah Miller** to be identified as author of this work has been asserted by the author in accordance with sections 77 and 78 of the Copyright, Designs and Patents Act 1988.

All rights reserved. No part of this publication may be reproduced, stored in a retrieval system, or transmitted in any form or by any means, electronic, mechanical, photocopying, recording, or otherwise, without the prior permission of the publishers.

Any person who commits any unauthorised act in relation to this publication may be liable to criminal prosecution and civil claims for damages.

A CIP catalogue record for this title is available from the British Library.

ISBN 9781398454415 (Paperback)
ISBN 9781398462816 (ePub e-book)

www.austinmacauley.com

First Published 2023
Austin Macauley Publishers Ltd®
1 Canada Square
Canary Wharf
London
E14 5AA

To my two little robots, Darryl and Ellie.

In a land called Storyburgh, not far from where you stay, lives a little robot called Beep. He stays with his mummy in a pretty toy box with all his friends nearby. Beep is a special robot; his mummy tells him all the time. He likes to do things in a certain way, in a certain order. His mummy helps him do this every day.

In the morning, he wakes up to the sound of his owl alarm clock. Mummy then comes in with a big smile and says, "Good morning, sleepy head, time to get out of bed". He knows he can get up now and get his breakfast; cereal with milk, up to the teddies top button on his bowl. Then Mummy puts blanket buddy on his chair so he can pick him up on the way out the door.

Today is a play day. Beep is excited he is going to meet his friends. Mummy says sometimes he gets too excited. They are meeting at the park. Beep likes the park but he has got to go in the small gate because the big gate frightens him, but it's alright because Mummy knows this. As they walk in, Beep spots his friends, Squeak, Roar and Melody and runs straight to them. He sometimes forgets Mummy doesn't like him to run off without her.

His friends are playing in the sandpit with some cars. "Can I play too?" asks Beep.

"Yes, here's a car to bury in the sand," replies Squeak.

But Beep doesn't want to bury his car in the sand, it will get all dirty and sandy. He just wants to spin the wheels and watch them going round and round.

"Come on, Beep, put the car in the sand and then drive it out like us," said Melody.

"No, I don't want to. It will get all sandy," cries Beep.

"So! It doesn't matter," says Roar, "but if you don't want to play, then that's fine." Roar dives in the sand with Squeak and Melody. This makes Beep feel sad because he did want to play but not the same way as the others.

That night as Mum was putting Beep to bed, he started to cry.

"What's wrong, my boy, why are you upset?"

"Mummy, I'm different from my friends. I think I need re-wired," Beep cried.

"Well of course you are different from your friends and they are different from you. We are all different from each other. You certainly don't need re-wired; you are who you are meant to be," soothed Mum.

Next morning was a nursery day which Beep enjoyed as long as he had blanket buddy with him. He says goodbye to Mummy and gives her a handshake to say goodbye because he doesn't like cuddles.

He then goes to his favourite place in the nursery called puzzle table, full of jigsaws and numbers. His friend Roar is already there and he is crying.

"What's wrong?" asks Beep quietly.

"I'm so silly. I can't finish this jigsaw puzzle because it's too difficult," cried Roar.

"I can help you if you want," replied Beep.
"That would be great," says Roar.

Beep puts all the shapes in a row so he can see them better. He then starts putting the shapes in the spaces in the right order. Roar claps his hands.

"Beep, you are so clever. I wish I could do puzzles like you."

"I could show you how to do another one if you like," says Beep shyly.

"OK, let's go," shouts Roar with excitement. "You are the smartest robot ever."

Beep smiles and says, "I'm just me."

THE END

Printed in the USA
CPSIA information can be obtained
at www.ICGtesting.com
LVHW060845140124
768768LV00022B/214